INVENTING PERFUME

by Emma Carlson Berne

Consultant: Beth Gambro
Reading Specialist, Yorkville, Illinois

Bearcub Books, an imprint of Bearport Publishing by FlutterBee

Teaching Tips

Before Reading

- Look at the cover of the book. Discuss the picture and the title.
- Ask readers to brainstorm a list of what they already know about perfume. What can they expect to see in the book?
- Go on a picture walk, looking through the pictures to discuss vocabulary and make predictions about the text.

During Reading

- Read for purpose. Encourage readers to think about what led to the desire for perfume as they are reading.
- Ask readers to look for the details of the book. What are some of the first uses for scents and perfume?
- If readers encounter an unknown word, ask them to look at the sounds in the word. Then, ask them to look at the rest of the page. Are there any clues to help them understand?

After Reading

- Encourage readers to pick a buddy and reread the book together.
- Ask readers to name two things that happened as perfume was being invented. Find the pages that tell about these things.
- Ask readers to write or draw something they learned about perfume.

Credits
Cover and title page, © Anna Solovei/iStock; 3, © marilyn barbone/Shutterstock; 5, © JackF/Adobe Stock; 7, © vectorlight/Shutterstock and © durmus1986/Shutterstock; 9, © Art_Pictures/Shutterstock; 11, © Sepia Times/Getty Images; 13, © Zev Radovan/Alamy Stock Photo; 14–15, © Valentina_G/Shutterstock; 17, © Science History Images/Alamy Stock Photo; 19, © Svittlana/iStock; 21, © SolStock/iStock; 22T, © Katarzyna Ledwon/Shutterstock; 22M, © Slaven Vlasic/Getty Images; 22B, © Suvorov_Alex/Shutterstock; 23TL, © Rabizo Anatolii/Shutterstock; 23TM, © Olga Miltsova/Shutterstock; 23TR, © buritora/Shutterstock; 23BL, © Print Collector/Getty Images; 23BM, © Marc Bruxelle/Shutterstock; 23BR, © bymuratdeniz/iStock.

See BearportPublishing.com for our statement on Generative AI Usage.

Library of Congress Cataloging-in-Publication Data is available at www.loc.gov or upon request from the publisher.

ISBN: 979-8-89577-588-2 (hardcover)
ISBN: 979-8-89577-768-8 (paperback)
ISBN: 979-8-89577-676-6 (ebook)

For more information, write to Bearport Publishing, 3500 American Blvd W, Suite 150, Bloomington, MN 55431.
Printed in the United States of America.

Contents

A Sweet Smell

Sniff, sniff!

I like this smell.

It makes me think of flowers.

But where did perfume come from?

Say perfume like PUR-fyoom

People have long used **scents**.

This started about 4,000 years ago.

In Mesopotamia, people used them to **honor** their gods.

They did this in Egypt, too.

Say Mesopotamia like *me*-suh-puh-TAY-mee-uh

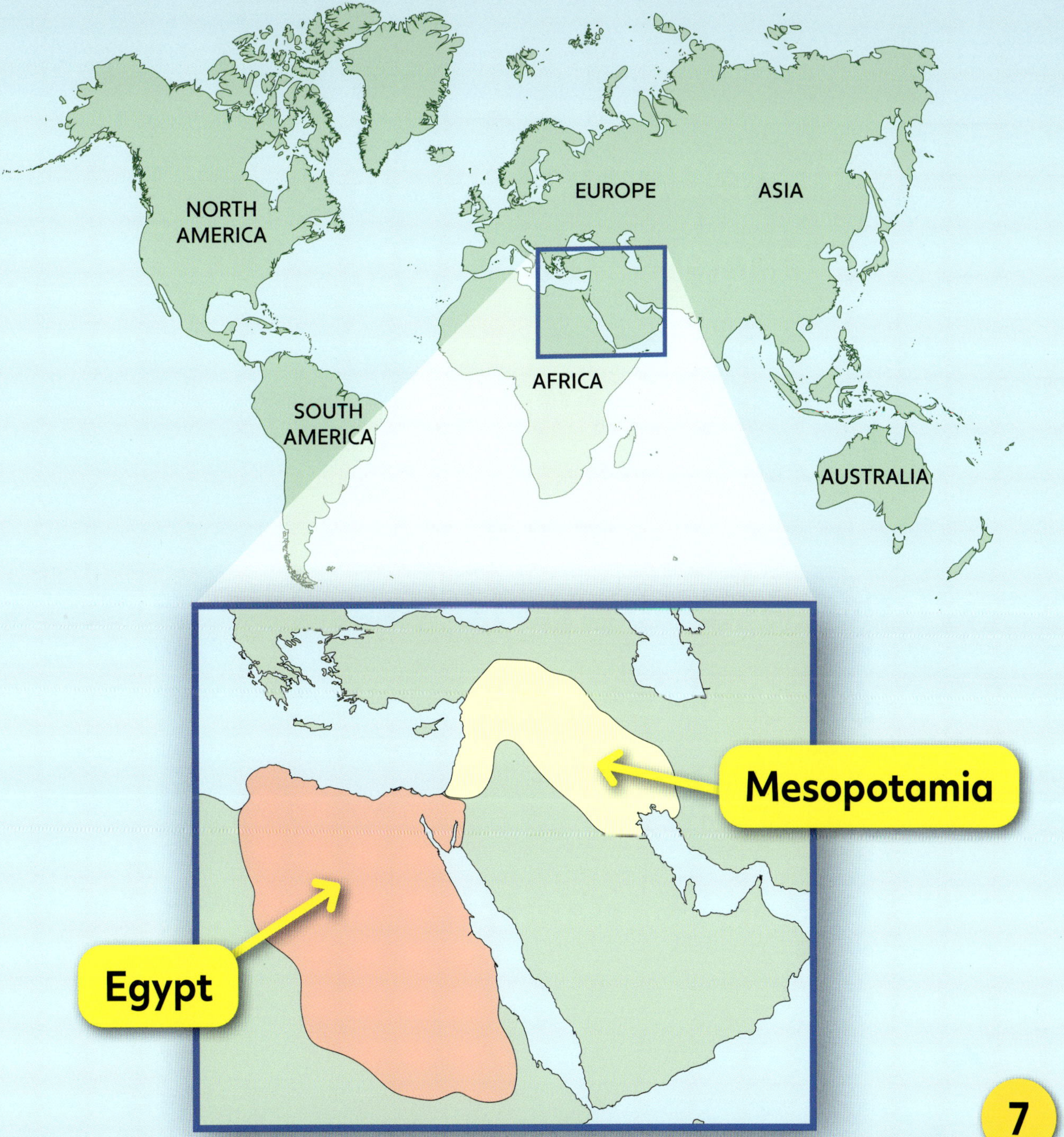
NORTH AMERICA
EUROPE
ASIA
AFRICA
SOUTH AMERICA
AUSTRALIA
Mesopotamia
Egypt

Some people burned wood and tree **sap**.

The smoke smelled good.

In fact, the word *perfume* comes from this.

It means through smoke.

People made oils that smelled nice, too.

They used the oils to get clean.

The first perfume maker lived about 3,200 years ago.

Her name was Tapputi.

She told others what she did.

Writing about Tapputi

Tapputi used science to make the scents.

She put flowers and **herbs** together.

Then, she added oil and water.

Next, Tapputi **filtered** the mix.

Drip, drip, drip.

This made the smell nicer.

It lasted longer, too.

Finally, she had perfume!

Over time, people used perfumes for more reasons.

They were not just for **religion** or cleaning.

People wore them because they liked the smells.

We still use perfumes today.

They come in thousands of different scents.

Some smell sweet.

Others are woody.

What is your favorite smell?

Great Offers

Fun Perfume Facts

There are more than 56,000 types of perfume in the world!

Perfumes can cost a lot. Some even sell for more than $1,000,000 per bottle!

One popular smell in perfumes comes from whales. Another is made from deer.

Glossary

filtered cleaned by removing small bits

herbs plants used for their taste or smell

honor to show great respect

religion a set of beliefs, often used to show respect for a god or gods

sap a liquid found in trees

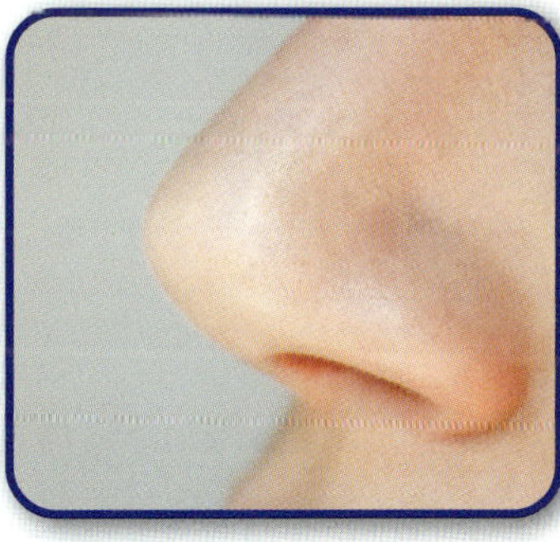

scents things that can be smelled

Index

Read More

Boothroyd, Jennifer. *Smelling (It Makes Sense!).* Minneapolis: Bearport Publishing, 2025.

Leed, Percy. *The Sense of Smell: A First Look (Read About Senses).* Minneapolis: Lerner Publications, 2023.

Learn More Online

1. Go to **FactSurfer.com** or scan the QR code below.
2. Enter "**Inventing Perfume**" into the search box.
3. Click on the cover of this book to see a list of websites.

About the Author

Emma Carlson Berne is the author of many books. She lives in Cincinnati, Ohio, with her husband, three children, one grumpy cat, and one friendly cat.